D0345514

HOW TO MAKE YOUR MAN BEHAVE

IN *21* DAYS

Or Less, Using

THE

SECRETS

OF

Professional DOG TRAINERS

Written By
Karen Salmansohn
Illustrated By
Alison Seiffer

Workman Publishing New York

Library of Congress Cataloging-in-Publication Data

Salmansohn, Karen.
How to make your man behave in 21 days or less using the secrets of
professional dog trainers/
written by Karen Salmansohn; illustrated by Alison Seiffer.
p. cm.
ISBN-13: 978-1-56305-626-0
1. Men – Humor. 2. Dog-Training – Humor.
I. Title.
PN6231 .M45S24 1994
818'.5402–dc20   94–4018 CIP

Workman books are available at special discounts
when purchased in bulk for premiums and sales promotions
as well as for fundraising or educational use.
Special editions can also be created to specification. For details,
contact the Special Sales Director at the address below.

Workman Publishing Company, Inc..
225 Varick Street
New York, NY 10014

Manufactured in the United States of America

First printing April 1994

16

CONTENTS

INTRODUCTION

It's been said in passing: **men are dogs**. Well, I believe there's much capital-"T" Truth behind this carelessly tossed-around bit of wisdom. I should know. I've spent exhaustive years of research – and exhausting hours involved in various forms of petting – only to prove (and reprove) my **Dog/Man Zen Belief System.** So, if you're not pleased with the way your man is behaving, I suggest you follow the advice of professionals – professional dog trainers, that is.

But, before we begin, let's get acquainted with this easy-to-follow key.

Easy-to-Follow Key

Dog = Man

Doggie = Man

Puppy = Man

Mongrel = Man

Canine = Man

Mutt = Man

Pack of Dogs = Men

Memorize this chart. Okay. Now you're better prepared to understand this book – and life.

Doggie
"Do"s & Don'ts

Consistently, a dog is "nicest" when he wants to be fed. Then he becomes **all wags and licks**. A known trick for keeping a dog on his best behavior is to just fill his bowl halfway so he's always yearning for more.

6

Same goes for his appetite for affection. Keep him in **constant emotional hunger** for you and he'll be more attentive and easier to control.

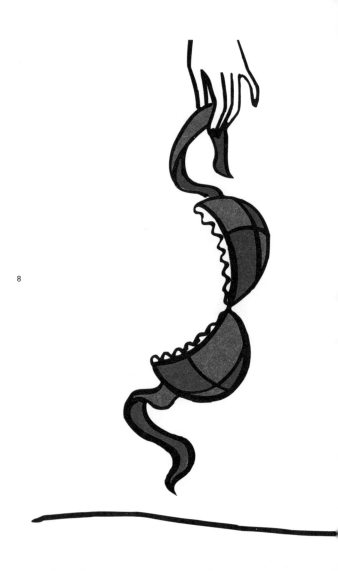

8

Memorize this very important fact
about **"Flight and Chase Behavior."**
If your dog is running away from you, the
worst thing you can do is chase after him.
He'll only run faster. Instead, remain
calm. Do something interesting to catch
his attention. Flaunt a colorful **plaything**.
Act like you're having loads of fun
without him. Soon he'll be trotting
eagerly back.

Be sure to introduce your dog very *slowly* into the various aspects of your life, or else you could inspire some very neurotic frenzied behavior; i.e., he could get **destructive** and break something.

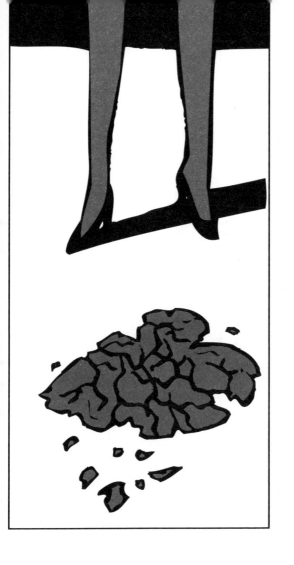

Until trust is built,
keep him on a **leash.**

Progressively lengthen it
as your trust grows.

And if that trust is questioned...

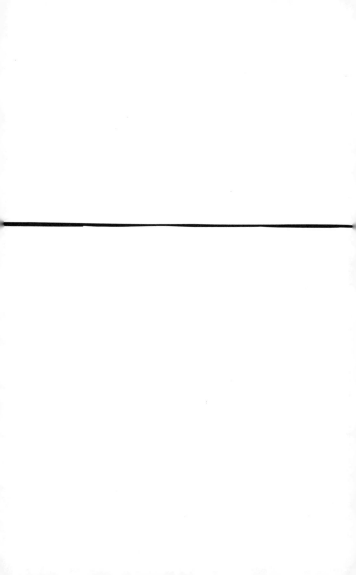

advance to a **choke collar.**

NOTE: Do *not* lose the leash until you're completely confident of your established **bond.**

17

Communicate your love with touch.

Gentle strokes and playful petting
are **positive motivational techniques**
for instilling good behavior.

Always say

No clearly,

so there's no mistaking

what you mean. In

time, you should be

able to communicate

your inner thoughts

with a simple look.

Never wait to act on **punishment.** To communicate effectively, you must punish directly after the misbehavior; i.e., immediately rub his nose in the mess he's made. No doubt about it. Next time he'll think twice before giving you shit.

From day one, you must **seize the leadership role**. Remain tough. Never be extra-nice to a dog who's misbehaving in hopes of winning him over. You must **refuse to pet or play** with a disobedient dog – resisting the lure of his puppy dog eyes. He'll get the hint **who's boss**.

Remember: **puppy love fades**. For instance, in those first 2–3 weeks of getting to know your dog, you might be charmed by the way he wakes you up at 6 A.M. with enthusiastic licking and slobbering, overcome by desire for you. But chances are, by the 4th week you'll prefer to wait till noon to get a pulse on his love for you. So think ahead. Do not allow **frivolous habits** to form in those first few weeks, or later your dog won't understand why you *suddenly* don't think it's precious when he starts nuzzling you in front of guests.

Dogs are known for **begging** and **panting** after things they're not allowed to have. Of course, it's best to keep objects of temptation out of sight, but unfortunately this is not always possible.

Luckily there's a training technique to discourage wayward behavior. Familiarize your dog with the following equation:

Forbidden Temptation = Intense Emotional Pain

Be consistent with your **house rules**.
You must decide once and for all:
do you or *don't you* like how
protectively he acts
whenever anyone visits –
or even approaches you?
And *do you* or *don't you* find it
adorable when he **plays with his
food?** Don't waver in your opinion,
or you'll lose your authority. And if
he doubts your authority even once,
he'll forever take advantage.

Don't make a habit

of yelling, or in time he'll

never listen to anything you say.

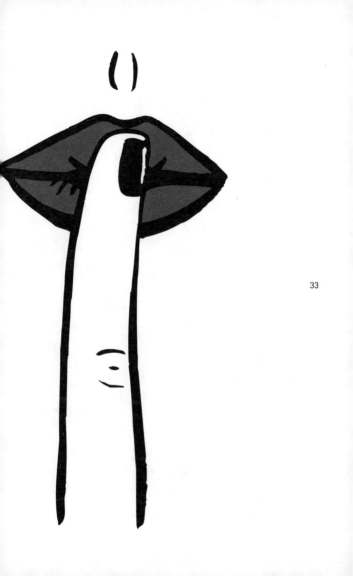

The most effective method for making

a dog do what you want is still

the old-fashioned reward system.

First find out what your dog's favorite

treats are. Then promise him one of

these treats if he does what he's told.

Make sure

he begs a lot for it first.

NOTE: The **extra begging** won't

help train him any better,

but it's fun to watch.

Remember

the

FOUR

Cs

ALWAYS BE:

Consistent...

about your demands;

Clear...

in how you express yourself;

Confident...

in your authority;

COMPLIMENTARY...

about good behavior.

42

Never treat aggression with more aggression – you'll only aggravate the situation. Always strive for **partnership** and **understanding.**

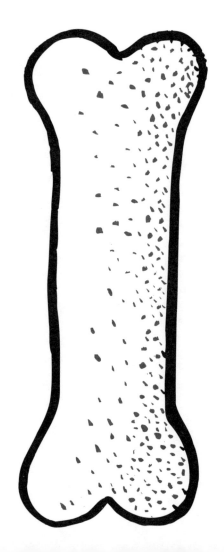

DOGGIE DOGMAS

Kind of uncanny how the
average canine and the **average man**
respond to the same training, isn't it?
Well, these shared training techniques work
because dog and man have characteristics
in common. I believe dog is man's best friend
for very deep psychological reasons.
Consider the following:

Dogs are known for their
pack behavior. A dog forced
to spend too much time in captivity
with you will suffer greatly.
He'll whine and bark until he's
let out to hang with his pack.

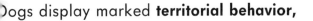Dogs display marked **territorial behavior,**

claiming their perceived space with
belongings and scent.

Dogs are
known
for **bad**
peeing
habits.

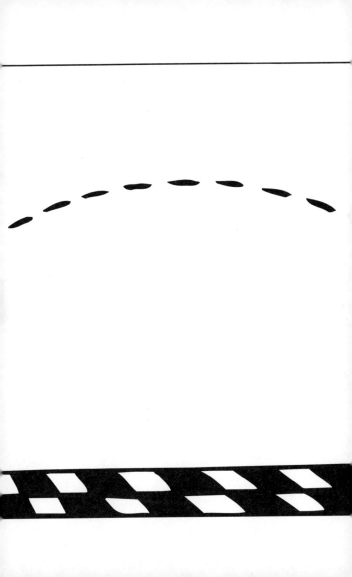

Plus, it is difficult to train a
dog to **put things back** where he
originally found them.

A dog's **first greeting** involves checking out the other's private parts in order to determine how friendly he wants to be.

Long courting periods

are not required

before he'll wanna start **humpin**

It's pointless to compete for attention with
a dog caught up in a ball game.
He is a **mindless, obsessed animal**.

A dog believes there's no such thing as spending too much time catering to one's **genitalia.**

Dogs are not especially known for their **grooming skills** or **cleanliness.**

A dog is naturally **protective.***

*WARNING: However, a dog is also
known to bite the very hand that feeds him.

No matter what a dog's God-given stature, he'll tend to think he's **bigger** than he truly is.

Dogs like to **eat** out of your plate.

No matter how
attached he is, a dog
will have the occasional
urge to stray.

One of a dog's favorite games is:

"Where Can I Hide My Big **Bone**?"

Dog Catching

Good News. Professional dog trainers believe you can determine from the start if a dog will make a good lifelong companion for **you**. But only if you ask the right questions — up front. So before you bring that man home with you, make sure you know how you feel about the following:

Does **size** matter? If so,
which do you prefer:

Giant?

Large?

Medium?

Small?

Tiny?

What are your **social needs** for the dog?
Do you want him to be:

Good with children?

Reserved with strangers?

Friendly with everyone?

Highly protective?

Just for show purposes?

For some it's not size
but **energy level** that counts.
Do you prefer a dog who is:

Vigorous and rough?

Playful?

Gentle and slow?

**In constant need
of exercise?**

Do you prefer a
dog who **barks**:

Rarely?

All the time?

Only on command?

What kind of **breeding** does the dog have? If possible, meet the dog's mom and get a sense of what she's like. Well-mannered? A yapper? A snob? Chances are, her offspring will behave similarly.

How does the dog **interact** with other dogs?

Is he a leader? An instigator? A loner?

Dominant or submissive? In all likelihood,

he'll manifest the same behavioral traits

in his relationship with you.

Ｈow old is the dog? Remember, **the older the dog, the harder to train**. He's probably already had years of negative reinforcement, and is now either spoiled or suffering from neglect.

What is your dog's **health** history like?

Unless he's a puppy, you never know where he's been. Play it safe. Have your dog tested by a doctor before you get too close.

DOGGIE
STYLES

Never pick a dog solely on looks or
because his particular breed is popular
with your friends. Remember, what's most
important is the dog's intrinsic personality
and temperament. Basically, there are
5 Personality/Temperament Categories
to choose from. Select the one that best
satisfies your needs and lifestyle.

THE SPORTING DOG

requires a lot of daily exercise;

is unhappy if kept indoors;

gets bored easily;

needs lots of attention;

likes to play games with you.

THE WORKING DOG

is bred to be strong and hearty;

has a highly developed

sense of property

ownership; is very territorial

and protective over whoever

takes him home; tends to be

quiet, independent

and antisocial.

86

THE TERRIER

is feisty, persistent and aggressive; makes a very loyal companion; has a tendency to try to dominate. You should consider how much time and energy you're willing to put into a relationship before you let this demanding kind of dog come home with you.

THE HOUND,

a hunter by nature,
is instinctually driven
to chase and
catch nearly anything
that moves;
has great stamina;
tends to be very
noisy and playful.

THE TOY DOG,

bred mainly for show,

is quite attention-getting

in appearance; tends to be

as loving with others

as he is with those

who take care of him;

often inspires strangers

to want to pet him;

usually on the skittish side.

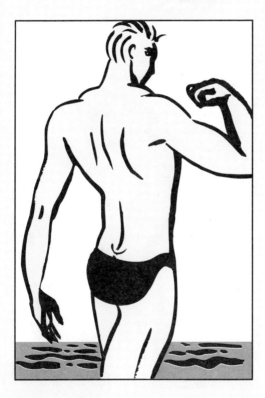

OUTRODUCTION

I know, I know, all this Dog/Man Psychology can be quite disturbing…especially if you're a man. But if you're a woman, you should be feeling a sense of…well, **hope.** Because once you understand how an animal thinks, the better you can communicate with him and the more responsive he'll be to your commands.

Those of you who wisely apply these **Dog/Man Psychology Tips** are guaranteed to see results *within 21 days.* Soon your man will be obediently **fetching** your morning paper and cappuccino, and **begging** you for more of whatever scraps of affection you care to offer him. Yes, I stalwartly believe both dog and man can be a woman's best friend—that is, with the right training and a lot of patience.